MONSTER

by
Walter Dean Myers

Student Packet

Written by
Pat Watson

Edited by
Katherine E. Martinez

Contains masters for:

2 Prereading Activities
1 Study Guide (5 pages)
5 Vocabulary Activities
5 Literary Analysis Activities
3 Comprehension Activities
5 Unit Quizzes
2 Final Tests (two levels)

Plus Detailed Answer Key

Note

The hardcover edition of this book, published by HarperCollins Publishers, ©1999, was used to prepare this guide. The page references may differ in other editions.

Please note: Parts of this novel deal with sensitive, mature issues. Please assess the appropriateness of this book for the age level and maturity of your students prior to reading and discussing it with your class.

ISBN 1-58130-689-X

Printed in the United States of America.

To order, contact your local school supply store, or—

Novel Units, Inc.
P.O. Box 97
Bulverde, TX 78163-0097

Web site: www.educyberstor.com

Name ______________________________

Directions: Rate each of the following statements before you read the novel and discuss your ratings with a partner. After you have completed the novel, rate and discuss the statements again.

1 ——— 2 ——— 3 ——— 4 ——— 5 ——— 6
strongly agree ... strongly disagree

	Before	**After**
1. For most teenagers, peer pressure supercedes parental influence.	_____	_____
2. Only "bad" kids get in serious trouble with the law.	_____	_____
3. The toughest judge a person faces is himself or herself.	_____	_____
4. If a victim is killed during a robbery, every person, from the lookout to the one who actually pulls the trigger, is mutually guilty.	_____	_____
5. People will lie to a judge and jury to save themselves.	_____	_____
6. A lawyer needs to have absolute confidence in the innocence of his or her client.	_____	_____
7. Guards in a jail are committed to protecting the inmates.	_____	_____
8. Poor schoolwork is a key indicator of crime-prone teenagers.	_____	_____
9. Criminal teenagers come from dysfunctional homes.	_____	_____
10. A person can be morally guilty even when found legally innocent.	_____	_____

Name ______________________________

Be a Detective!

Directions: Check out the book by looking at the cover and thumbing through the pages. Then, ask yourself Who? What? Where? When? Why? and How? Write your questions in the spaces below. Exchange your paper with a partner and answer each other's questions.

How?

____
____
____
____

Who?

____
____
____
____

Where?

____
____
____
____

Why?

____
____
____
____

What?

____
____
____
____

When?

____
____
____
____

Name ______________________________

Directions: Write an answer to each question on separate paper. Thought or opinion questions are starred. Use your answers during class discussion, for writing assignments, or to review for tests. Complete the activities as assigned by the teacher.

Pages 1-19

1. Identify the narrator and tell how old he is. Where is he and how long has he been there? How does he feel about his life at this point?
2. *Why does he decide to make a movie? What would you do in a similar situation?
3. Why does the narrator name his movie script *Monster*?
4. Of what crime is Steve accused? What reflects the seriousness of his circumstances?
5. Activity: Write a metaphor or simile poem about FEAR.

Pages 20-43

1. What is the exact nature of the crime and who is accused of participating in the actual robbery and murder? What is the role Steve allegedly played?
2. Why are cigarettes a key issue for the prosecution?
3. *What is Zinzi's reason for informing? How do both Briggs and O'Brien cast doubt on his testimony? If you were a juror, would you believe him?
4. What is the purpose of the flashback on pp. 41-43?
5. Activity: Explain your reaction to the maxim, "Innocent until proven guilty" in a paragraph or poem.

Pages 45-58

1. *Summarize Steve's feelings about jail. How would you feel if you were Steve?
2. Identify Bolden and tell what you learn about him from the testimony.
3. *What do you learn from the flashback on pp. 49-51? Why do you think this is important to the plot?
4. *If you were a juror, what impact would Bolden's testimony have on you?

Pages 59-88

1. Why does Steve think the prosecution calls on witnesses such as Zinzi and Bolden?
2. *Explain Steve's dream. Why do you think this is significant?

Name ________________________________

3. *Note the commonality of events in the midst of Steve's life/death trial (pp. 65-66). Explain a time in your life when you resented "life as usual" when you were experiencing personal trauma.
4. Summarize Detective Karyl's testimony.
5. How did the detective trace the crime to Bobo Evans, James King, and Steve Harmon?
6. Why does O'Brien say the trial could be going better?
7. *Identify Osvaldo Cruz and summarize his incriminating testimony. Would you believe him? Why or why not?

Pages 89-113

1. *Summarize Steve's journal entry on pp. 89-98. What impact do you think the trial has on the junior high students who attend?
2. What effect do the pictures of the crime scene have on Steve? Why does Steve think O'Brien shows the pictures to him?
3. What roles did Osvaldo and Steve allegedly play in the crime?
4. *What choice does Briggs say Osvaldo has been given by the prosecutor? What impression of Osvaldo do you have based on his testimony?
5. What does O'Brien reveal about Osvaldo during her cross-examination of him? What effect does this have on at least one juror?
6. *Explain why you do or do not think Steve's father believes in his innocence.
7. Activity: Bring to class newspaper or magazine articles about teen gangs. In an oral discussion, compare your findings with what Osvaldo reveals about the Diablos.

Pages 115-126

1. How does O'Brien think the case is going for Steve? Why?
2. Explain how Steve first hears public news about the crime and the effect it has on him.
3. Give the details of the crime according to the newscaster.
4. *What impact does Steve's predicament have on his family? Refer to his father's visit in jail and the effect of his arrest on his mother and brother. How would your family react in a similar situation?
5. Activity: Complete the following: GUILT is... INNOCENCE is...

Name ______________________________

Pages 127-151

1. *What "cheap trick" does Petrocelli use? What effect do you think this will have on the jurors?
2. *Why does Steve feel he loses his identity in jail? Identify a time in your life when you felt you were losing your own identity.
3. According to his journal entry, what causes Steve to get involved with the others in planning the robbery?
4. What was the ultimate cause of Nesbitt's death?
5. Explain Steve's conversation with O'Brien and why he is troubled.
6. *How does Steve view guilt? Explain why you agree or disagree with him.
7. Explain what happens when Steve's mother visits him and the effect it has on Steve.
8. Activity: Write a metaphor or simile poem about LONELINESS.

Pages 153-171

1. Explain Steve's analysis of why there are so many fights in jail.
2. What is ironic about Steve's being in jail?
3. *What is Lorelle Henry's role for the prosecution? How would you evaluate the impact of her testimony?
4. How does Briggs attempt to discredit Henry's testimony?
5. Why does Lorelle Henry have trouble testifying?
6. Activity: Write a letter from Steve to Jerry after Jerry visits him outside the jail.

Pages 172-200

1. Why is Bobo Evans' appearance in the courtroom prejudicial? What is the judge's reaction to the defense counsel's objection?
2. *Where is Bobo Evans incarcerated? For how long? Why? What are other crimes for which he has been arrested? Do you think his testimony is valid? Why or why not?
3. Describe and interpret Bobo's account of the crime. Does he imply the shooting was intentional or accidental?
4. *How does Briggs portray Bobo? Explain why you do or do not agree with him.
5. Activity: Write a name poem for Bobo Evans.

Name ______________________________

Pages 201-214

1. What does O'Brien hope to do for Steve's defense? What does Briggs hope to do for King's defense?
2. *Explain how Steve feels after Bobo's testimony and why he feels this way.
3. *Who does Briggs call as King's first defense witness? What is her testimony? Do you think she is an effective witness?
4. *Why is George Nipping called to testify? Explain why you think his testimony will or will not help King's defense.
5. Activity: Make a list of people you most admire. Choose one and write a short poem about or a letter to him or her.

Pages 215-237

1. *What does O'Brien advise Steve to do? Do you think her advice is valid? Why or why not?
2. *Summarize Steve's testimony. Explain whether or not you think the jury will believe him.
3. Why isn't Briggs going to put King on the stand in his own defense?
4. *According to O'Brien, when do closing arguments win court cases? Why do you think she says this?
5. What is Steve's view of truth? What are the inmates' views?
6. What two key points must be refuted if Steve has a chance to be acquitted?
7. *What is Steve's alibi for the day of the crime? Do you think this will or will not convince the jury of his innocence? Explain your answer.

Pages 238-253

1. How does Briggs characterize Bobo Evans?
2. List at least five key points from Briggs' summation.
3. List at least five key points from O'Brien's summation.
4. Activity: Write a note Steve's mother might write to him during a recess of the trial after O'Brien's summation.

Pages 254-281

1. List at least five key points from Petrocelli's summation for the prosecution.
2. *Explain why you think Steve's movie script shows George Washington's portrait, the New York state and American flags, the motto over the judge's desk, and the wall mural in the courtroom.
3. Explain what happens to each of the characters who are involved in the crime: Steve Harmon, James King, Bobo Evans, Osvaldo Cruz.
4. *What does Steve do following his acquittal? Why is this significant?
5. *Explain what you think O'Brien sees when she looks at Steve.

Name ______________________________

dispensary (2)	grainy (3)	obscene (7)	felony (12)
mentor (19)	safeguard (21)	merits (21)	infringing (21)
conspiracy (23)	impede (23)	redress (26)	lynch (26)
grandiose (27)	articulate (28)	inventory (31)	careens (42)
tentative (42)	drawl (50)	pertinent (55)	silhouetted (57)

Directions: Match each vocabulary word with the correct synonym.

____	1. dispensary	a. eloquent
____	2. grainy	b. worth
____	3. obscene	c. obstruct
____	4. felony	d. infirmary
____	5. mentor	e. accent
____	6. safeguard	f. appropriate
____	7. merits	g. crime
____	8. infringing	h. indecent
____	9. conspiracy	i. swerves
____	10. impede	j. protection
____	11. redress	k. advisor
____	12. lynch	l. encroaching
____	13. grandiose	m. rough, unrefined
____	14. articulate	n. kill
____	15. inventory	o. listing
____	16. careens	p. outlined
____	17. tentative	q. restitution
____	18. drawl	r. imposing
____	19. pertinent	s. careful
____	20. silhouetted	t. plot, intrigue

Name ______________________________

Monster
Activity #4 • Vocabulary
Pages 59–126

affidavit (66) pans (67) grotesque (68) pessimist (73)
lethal (73) grimaces (73) perpetrator (74) proposition (85)
juvenile (86) civil (88) judicial (97) apprehended (102)
ruffled (107) hexagon (110) cope (111) cacophony (117)
ghetto (120) dismay (121) glowers (123) precinct (124)

Directions: In the chart below, (1) place a check mark in the column that best describes your familiarity with the word; (2) find the sentence in which the word appears in the text of the novel; (3) look up each word in the dictionary to find the definition as used in the novel.

Word	Can define	Have seen or heard	Don't know
1. affidavit (66)			
2. pans (67)			
3. grotesque (68)			
4. pessimist (73)			
5. lethal (73)			
6. grimaces (73)			
7. perpetrator (74)			
8. proposition (85)			
9. juvenile (86)			
10. civil (88)			
11. judicial (97)			
12. apprehended (102)			
13. ruffled (107)			
14. hexagon (110)			
15. cope (111)			
16. cacophony (117)			
17. ghetto (120)			
18. dismay (121)			
19. glowers (123)			
20. precinct (124)			

Name ______________________________

arcs (130)	montage (131)	premises (131)	perimeter (133)
traversed (135)	trapezius (135)	wrenched (147)	mosaic (151)
whist (154)	diminutive (161)	sidebar (172)	prejudicial (173)
manslaughter (176)	parole (186)	concentric (199)	hurdy-gurdy (199)

Directions: If the italicized word is used correctly in the following sentences, check the "Yes" box. If it is used incorrectly, check the "No" box and reword the sentence to read correctly.

	Yes	No
1. The *arcs* of light traveled in a straight line.	______	______
2. The students created a *montage* to symbolize the theme of the novel.	______	______
3. A person has the right to establish rules for his own *premises.*	______	______
4. The *perimeter* identifies the depth of a figure.	______	______
5. Pioneers *traversed* the prairie in covered wagons.	______	______
6. The *trapezius* area of the body is in the leg.	______	______
7. The policeman gently *wrenched* the gun from the suspect.	______	______
8. Pieces of colored glass can be used to create a beautiful *mosaic.*	______	______
9. Playing *whist* requires a net and racket.	______	______
10. All professional basketball players are *diminutive.*	______	______
11. Officials in a trial ask for a *sidebar* for a private conference with the judge.	______	______
12. A *prejudicial* witness for the defense is expected to aid the defendant.	______	______
13. *Manslaughter* is premeditated murder.	______	______
14. Good behavior enhances a prisoner's chance for *parole.*	______	______
15. *Concentric* circles are formed around a common center.	______	______
16. *Hurdy-gurdy* music is usually heard in a church.	______	______

Name ________________________________

verge (203)	subdued (208)	condescendingly (209)	verify (210)
precisely (211)	access (214)	infer (215)	surly (215)
soliciting (231)	compassionate (235)	depicting (235)	vouch (236)

Directions: Match each vocabulary word with the correct antonym.

____	1. verge	a. disprove
____	2. subdued	b. friendly
____	3. condescendingly	c. inaccurately
____	4. verify	d. far away
____	5. precisely	e. deny
____	6. access	f. opposing
____	7. infer	g. restriction
____	8. surly	h. intense
____	9. soliciting	i. erasing
____	10. compassionate	j. prove
____	11. depicting	k. humbly
____	12. vouch	l. pitiless

Name ______________________________

implicates (239)	potential (242)	taint (243)	consigning (243)
indulgence (244)	elicit (245)	constitute (246)	alleged (249)
gullible (250)	acquit (253)	contention (255)	botched (259)
moral (261)	causative (262)	bravado (266)	dialog (271)
pensive (276)	reformatory (270)		

Directions: Fill in each blank in the following sentences with the correct vocabulary word.

1. ____________________ among different segments of society often leads to verbal or physical conflicts.
2. A person's reputation can ____________________ his credibility.
3. Someone who ____________________ another person involves him or her in the illegal action.
4. A ____________________ decision is based on honesty and virtue.
5. Juvenile offenders may spend years in a state ____________________.
6. Neglect is a ____________________ factor in some infant deaths.
7. A ____________________ person is easily led by someone with a dominant personality.
8. It is difficult to correct a ____________________ carpentry job.
9. A person may struggle for many years before reaching his or her full ____________________.
10. Reasonable doubt justifies a jury to ____________________ someone who is accused of a crime.
11. Conflicting testimony makes it difficult to ____________________ the truth during a trial.
12. ____________________ information involves handing it over to another person.
13. We often have ____________________ thoughts about events from the past.
14. Teenagers desire ____________________ from their parents and teachers.
15. ____________________ reflects more than one person's thoughts and/or opinions.
16. Discussing a crime does not ____________________ the commission of that crime.
17. People who are inwardly frightened often present an outward ____________________.
18. An ____________________ incrimination may be difficult to prove.

Name ______________________________

Attribute Web

Directions: Place Steve Harmon's name in the large center circle. In the blank smaller circles, fill in verbs. On the lines, supply words to follow each of the verbs. For example, a character might "need love."

Name ______________________________

Attribute Web

Directions: In the central oval, place "trial." Write each major character's name on the six long lines. Write each character's reaction to the trial on the smaller lines below his or her name.

Name ______________________________

Character Analysis Chart

Directions: List some of the characters who appear in *Monster* in the boxes below. Add to this chart as more characters are introduced. Working in small groups, discuss the attributes of the various characters with other members of your group. In each character's box, write several words or phrases you feel describe him or her.

Name ______________________________

Story Map

Directions: Select five important events from *Monster* to put into this flow chart. Be sure to choose carefully so that you will cover the plot in the book through the last chapter.

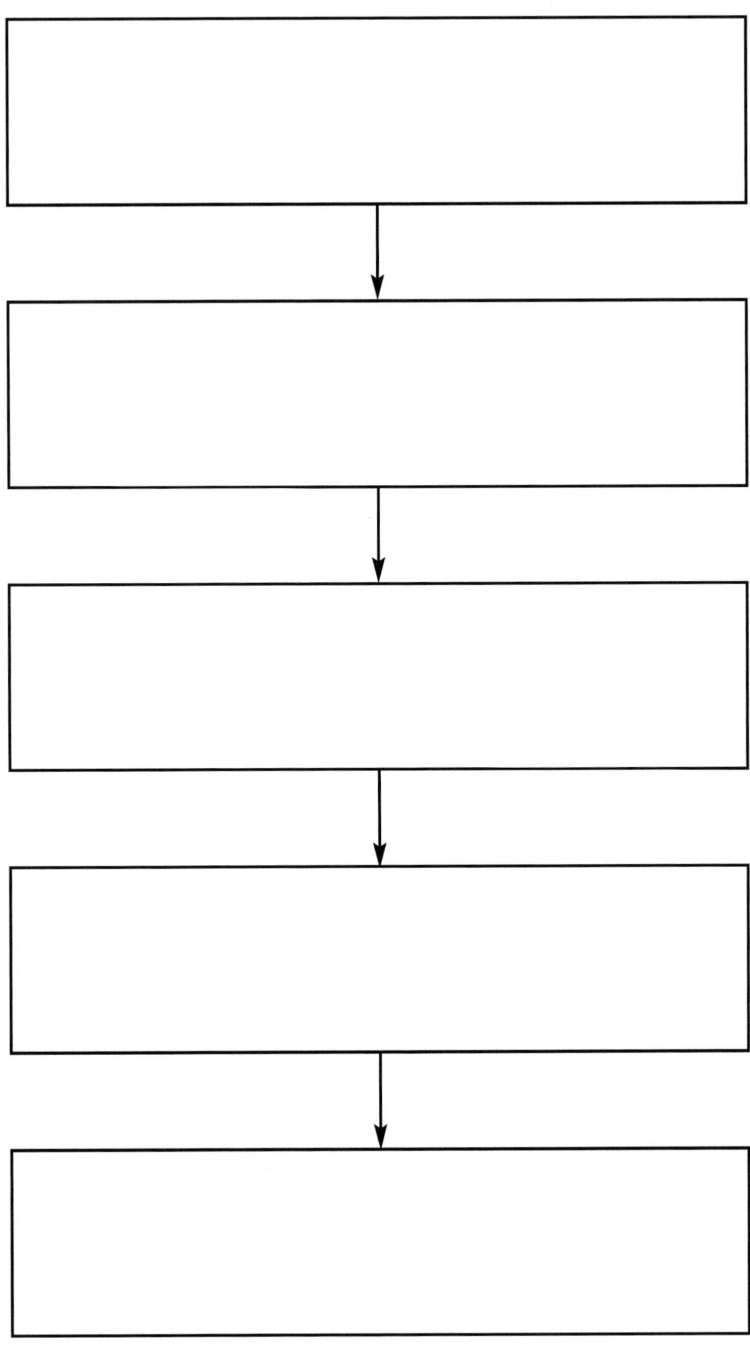

Name ______________________________

Novel Web Diagram

Directions: The oval is the place for the book's title. Fill in the boxes to summarize the story.

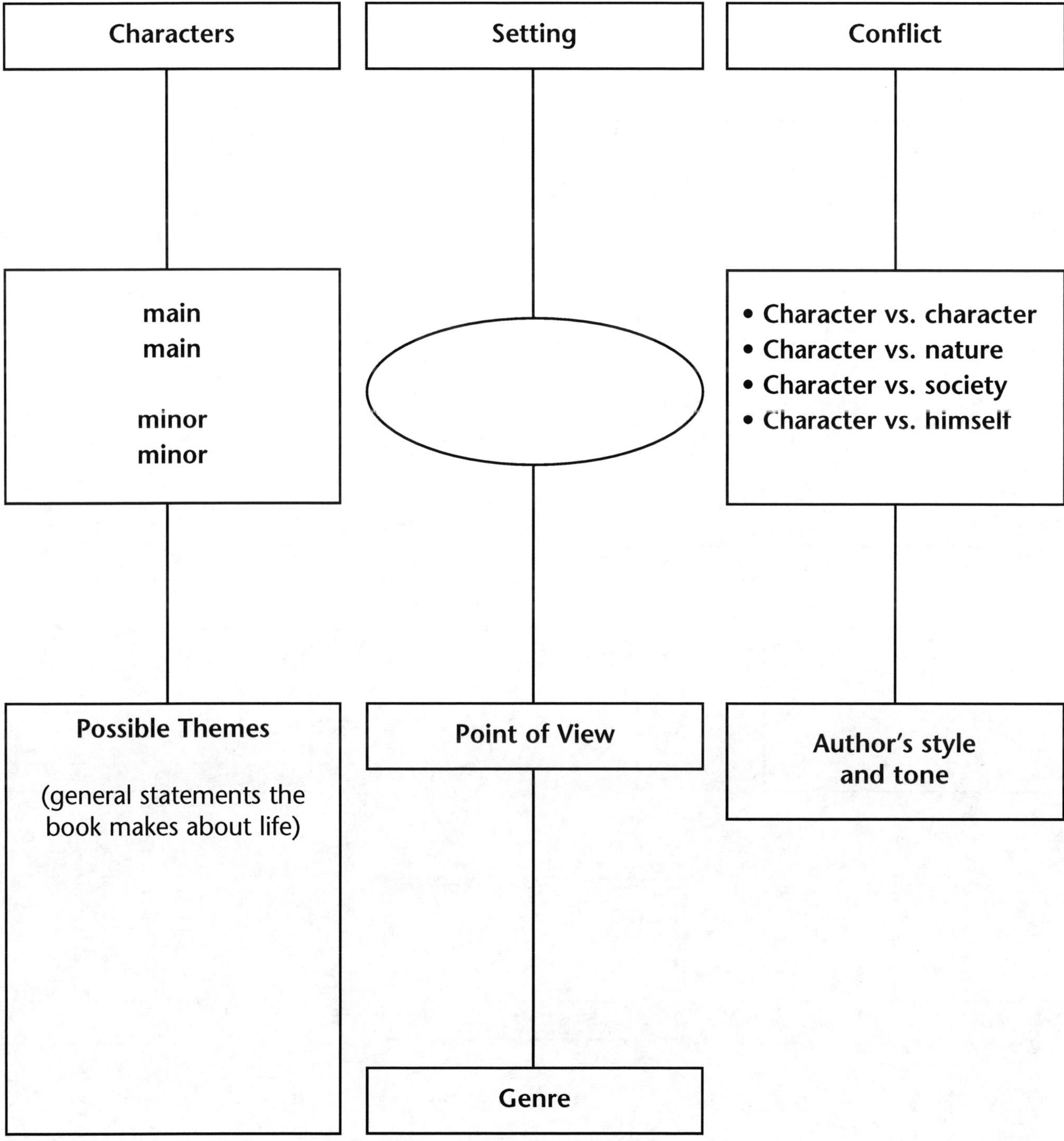

Name ______________________

Cause and Effect

Directions: Write one major effect of the events in *Monster* in the effect box. Then brainstorm all of the possible causes for the effect from information in the book. Fill in the boxes with both the cause and a brief explanation of why it relates to the effect.

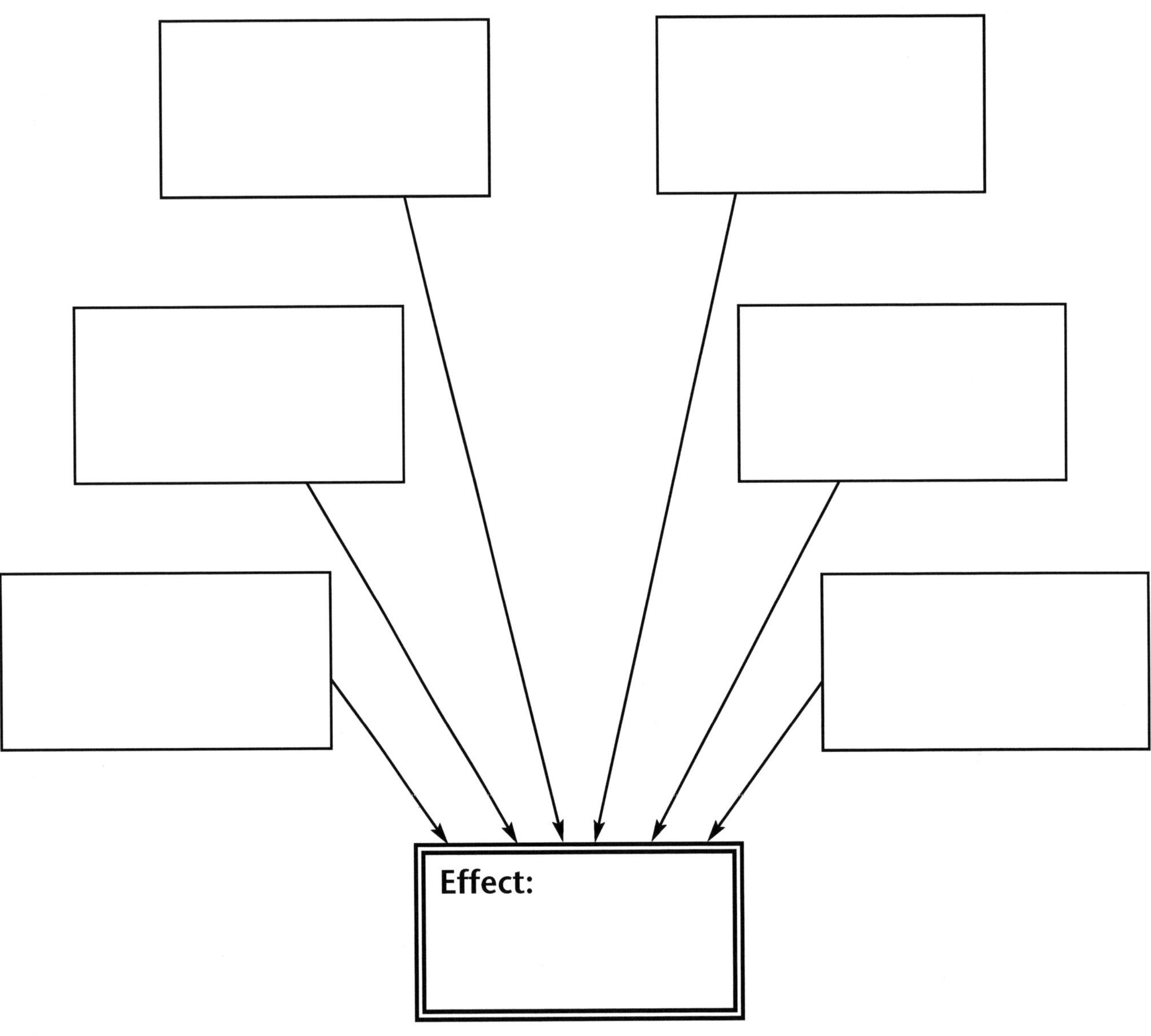

Name ________________________________

Making Decisions

Problem: Steve Harmon must decide whether or not to join King, Evans, and Cruz in the robbery.

Directions: Choose three to seven possible solutions to the stated problem.

(a) State each possible solution in a short sentence.
(b) Design three to five "criteria" (questions you can ask to measure how good a particular solution may be)
(c) Rate the criteria for each solution: 1=yes, 2=maybe, 3=no

SOLUTIONS ↓	CRITERIA				
1.					
2.					
3.					
4.					
5.					
6.					
7.					

Name ______________________________

Using Dialogue

Directions: Choose a section of dialogue from the book to analyze. Fill in the chart to describe and evaluate how dialogue is used in the story.

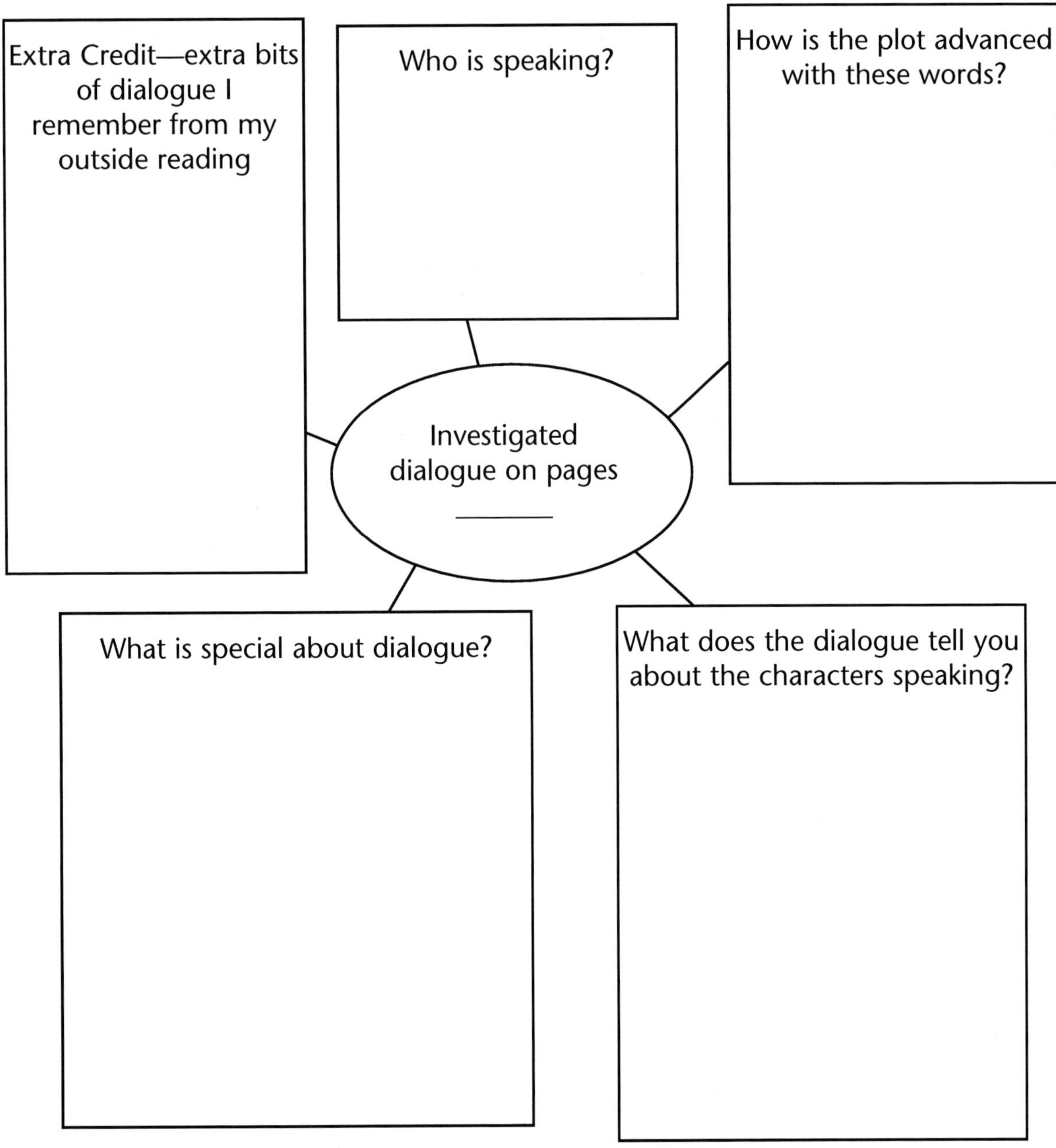

Name ________________________________

A. Match each character with the correct identification.

____ 1. Sandra Petrocelli

____ 2. Kathy O'Brien

____ 3. Steve Harmon

____ 4. Sal Zinzi

____ 5. Bobo Evans

a. narrator of the novel

b. participant in the crime; informs on the others

c. ties stolen cigarettes to the defendants

d. prosecuting attorney

e. defense attorney for narrator

B. True/False

____ 6. The first journal entries establish a mood of fear.

____ 7. The narrator decides to write a movie script about his experiences in order to prove his innocence.

____ 8. James King is the narrator's co-defendant.

____ 9. Bolden identifies Evans as one of the men involved in the crime.

____ 10. The perpetrators of the crime commit premeditated murder.

Name ______________________________

Fill in the blanks.

1. Steve Harmon feels that he has the word ____________________ tattooed on his forehead.

2. O'Brien feels that part of her job is to make Steve look __________________ in the eyes of the jury.

3. __________________________ accuses Steve of pulling the trigger.

4. O'Brien feels Steve's case is not going well because______________________________

   ____.

5. Three points against Steve are (name 2 of the 3) ______________________________

   ____.

6. Osvaldo Cruz is a member of the _____________________________ gang.

7. Cruz testifies that he participated in the crime because __________________________

   ____.

8. If convicted, Steve faces a possible sentence of _______________________________.

9. Cruz identifies Steve as the ____________________________ during the crime.

10. The defense attacks Cruz's credibility by (2 of 3)________________________________

    ____.

11. The detectives arrest Steve (place) ____________________________________.

Name ______________________________

A. True/False

____ 1. O'Brien accuses Petrocelli of using a "cheap trick" by showing the crime scene photos of Nesbitt just before the weekend.

____ 2. James King owns the gun used in the crime.

____ 3. Nesbitt died when the bullet pierced his brain.

____ 4. Steve's brother Jerry visits him in jail.

____ 5. Briggs questions Bobo's credibility by referring to him as a dope dealer and a thief.

B. Write short answers to the following questions.

6. How does Steve view his role in the crime?

7. What does Steve's mother tell him after she visits him in jail?

8. Why is Lorelle Henry a star witness for the prosecution?

9. Give three points from Bobo Evans' testimony for the prosecution.

10. What is Osvaldo Cruz's stated reason for participating in the crime?

Name ______________________________

A. Fill in the blanks.

1. When O'Brien has Steve write down people in his life whom he admires, he writes ______________________________ name twice.

2. Dorothy Moore's testimony in King's defense carries little weight because ______________________________.

3. O'Brien's advice to Steve is to ______________________________.

4. O'Brien prepares Steve for his testimony by ______________________________.

5. To O'Brien's questions about his involvement in the robbery, Steve replies ______________________________.

B. True/False

____ 6. The prosecution's strongest point against Steve is his connection to Evans.

____ 7. O'Brien believes cases are won on closing arguments only on television.

____ 8. Steve denies any acquaintance with any of those involved in the robbery.

____ 9. Steve's alibi for the day of the crime involves actually filming a school project.

____ 10. Mr. Sawicki considers Steve to be an honest young man.

Name ______________________________

Match each character with the correct statement.

A. Briggs B. O'Brien C. Petrocelli D. James King E. Steve Harmon

____ 1. compares Steve Harmon's character as opposed to that of Evans, Zinzi, and Cruz

____ 2. concludes summation with reference to Steve's moral decision to participate in the crime

____ 3. is haunted by thoughts of decisions he did or did not make

____ 4. places James King at the crime scene through the testimony of three witnesses

____ 5. contrasts reputation of a parade of prosecution witnesses with that of Dorothy Moore

____ 6. questions who he really is

____ 7. is found guilty of murder

____ 8. challenges Lorelle Henry's identification of King

____ 9. turns away from Steve after hearing the verdict

____ 10. is found not guilty

Name ______________________________

A. Identification: Match each character with the correct description. (1 pt. each)

____	1. Steve Harmon		a. 14 years old; member of Diablos; informant
____	2. James King		b. young, articulate store clerk; prosecution witness
____	3. Sandra Petrocelli		c. 23 years old; "thug"; co-defendant in trial
____	4. Kathy O'Brien		d. 55-year-old Black victim of robbery/murder
____	5. Bobo Evans		e. 16 years old; consumed with fear and regret
____	6. Osvaldo Cruz		f. defendant's mentor in film club; defense witness
____	7. Monster		g. intense, attractive; New York District Attorney
____	8. Lorelle Henry		h. prosecutor's pseudonym for defendant
____	9. José Delgado		i. petite, red-headed; doubts defendant's innocence
____	10. Asa Briggs		j. retired school librarian; witness for prosecution
____	11. Mr. Sawicki		k. attorney for narrator's co-defendant
____	12. Alguinaldo Nesbitt		l. big, mean, ugly; testifies in plea bargain arrangement

B. Multiple Choice: Choose the BEST answer. (2 pts. each)

13. The initial scene of *Monster* establishes a mood of
    (a) confidence
    (b) complacency
    (c) fear
    (d) courage

14. The movie script in *Monster* reflects Steve Harmon's
    (a) search for his true self
    (b) anger at the court system
    (c) rebellion toward his parents
    (d) dreams of college

15. O'Brien's first recorded advice to Steve is
    (a) to turn his life around
    (b) that he should listen to his parents
    (c) to be prepared for a prison sentence
    (d) that he had better take the trial very seriously

16. Steve Harmon has been charged with
    (a) robbery
    (b) felony murder
    (c) possession of drugs
    (d) breaking and entering

17. The prosecution claims that
    (a) Steve and Jerry killed a man
    (b) Steve and King planned the crime
    (c) Evans and King perpetrated the crime
    (d) Evans and Cruz perpetrated the crime

18. During the prosecutor's opening statements, Steve
    (a) falls asleep
    (b) writes the word "monster" over and over
    (c) writes the word "guilty" over and over
    (d) sits and cries

19. José Delgado's testimony revolves around
    (a) ownership of the gun
    (b) his whereabouts at the time of the crime
    (c) an eyewitness identity of the criminals
    (d) missing cartons of cigarettes

20. Zinzi testifies for the prosecution
    (a) in order to get out of jail early
    (b) because he was at the drugstore
    (c) because he was a friend of the victim
    (d) to ease his conscience

21. Bolden implicates Bobo Evans in the crime based on
    (a) the receipt of stolen money
    (b) Bolden's eyewitness account
    (c) what Cruz told him
    (d) Bolden's purchase of cigarettes from Evans

22. Steve's memories of home reveal
    (a) a drunken father
    (b) a single mother
    (c) neat, clean surroundings and a loving family
    (d) dirty, squalid surroundings

Name ______________________________

23. Steve feels that Petrocelli is using Zinzi and Bolden's testimonies to
    (a) remind the jury that he and King look just like them
    (b) detract the jury from the truth
    (c) keep Steve and King's images separate from Zinzi and Bolden
    (d) make the jury angry
24. Steve's experiences in prison typify
    (a) a plunge into "the real world"
    (b) taking on the characteristics of those we are around
    (c) hiding behind a façade of nonchalance
    (d) plans for revenge
25. Detective Karyl portrays Nesbitt as
    (a) an upright white citizen
    (b) a slothful businessman
    (c) a visionary who invited trouble
    (d) a hard-working, well-respected Black businessman
26. O'Brien tells Steve they must show that Petrocelli
    (a) is lying
    (b) hates young Black men
    (c) simply made a mistake
    (d) is looking for a scapegoat
27. A critical point the defense reveals about Osvaldo Cruz is that
    (a) he has lied about being a member of the Diablos gang
    (b) he holds a grudge against Steve
    (c) revenge is his motive for testifying
    (d) he doesn't even know Steve or King
28. As a witness for the prosecution, Osvaldo Cruz
    (a) denies knowing King
    (b) admits his part in the robbery
    (c) is considered a hostile witness
    (d) says Steve pulled the trigger
29. If convicted of the crime for which he is on trial, Steve Harmon faces
    (a) 25 years to life
    (b) 10 years probation
    (c) remaining in the reformatory until he is 18
    (d) 5 years

Name ______________________________

30. Steve had aligned himself with King, Evans, and Cruz because
    (a) they intimidated him
    (b) he wanted to earn some fast money
    (c) he wanted to be like them
    (d) they promised him drugs
31. Osvaldo Cruz's role in the robbery was to
    (a) act as the lookout
    (b) detain the clerk from entering the store
    (c) secure the gun
    (d) slow down anyone who came after King and Evans
32. Cruz's testimony reveals
    (a) the gang is forcing him to testify
    (b) the government has given him a deal
    (c) King offered him money not to testify
    (d) the detectives coerced a confession from him
33. When Steve's father visits him in jail, he reflects
    (a) sorrow
    (b) anger
    (c) hopelessness
    (d) apathy
34. Petrocelli attempts to impact the jury with the horror of the crime
    (a) by showing a surveillance video of the crime scene
    (b) through the testimony of the victim's son
    (c) by taking them to the crime scene
    (d) by the timing of showing them graphic pictures of the victim
35. Mr. Nesbitt died
    (a) from a knife wound to the heart
    (b) from a bullet wound to the brain
    (c) by drowning in his own blood
    (d) from a heart attack during the crime
36. In his journal, Steve describes his presence in the drugstore
    (a) by saying King's crime was much worse than his
    (b) by envisioning himself walking into the drugstore to look for mints, then walking out
    (c) by stating that he did not actually take part in the robbery
    (d) by reminding his attorney that it is a free country and he can go where he wishes

37. Steve's mother tries to encourage him by
    (a) bringing him art supplies
    (b) bringing him a Bible
    (c) telling him his grandfather is coming to see him
    (d) bringing his little brother to his cell
38. Lorelle Henry's testimony incriminates
    (a) Steve
    (b) Evans
    (c) Cruz
    (d) King
39. Briggs attacks Henry's testimony by
    (a) implying she was influenced by police through the manipulation of pictures
    (b) proving she is a habitual liar
    (c) questioning her sanity
    (d) proving she is related to the victim
40. Evans' testimony does all but which one of the following?
    (a) identifies Steve as a participant in the crime
    (b) accuses King of firing the shot
    (c) shows remorse that he killed a man
    (d) says that the murder was accidental
41. Evans agrees to testify against King and Steve
    (a) because he is repentant
    (b) in exchange for $10,000
    (c) after he sees the death photos of the victim
    (d) in a plea bargain for a lesser charge
42. Briggs attacks Evans' credibility by all but which one of the following?
    (a) says he is a thief
    (b) proves he took money for his testimony
    (c) portrays him as a man who can kill a man, then immediately go and eat
    (d) reveals him as a drug dealer
43. According to O'Brien, Evans' testimony
    (a) did not hurt Steve's case
    (b) slightly damaged Steve's case
    (c) was very detrimental to Steve's case
    (d) was obviously a lie

44. Steve's advice to Jerry would be to
    (a) join a gang for protection
    (b) always tell the truth
    (c) get an education
    (d) think about all the tomorrows of his life

45. Mr. Sawicki characterizes Steve as
    (a) an outstanding young man
    (b) a mediocre student
    (c) a dreamer who never completes a project
    (d) a weak but cooperative student

46. O'Brien's summation asserts that
    (a) the overpowering evidence points to King's guilt
    (b) the state has failed to prove Steve fired the gun
    (c) the state has failed to show any acquaintance of Steve with the others
    (d) the state has failed to place Steve at the crime scene through eyewitness testimony

47. Steve does not want to think about
    (a) his mother and father
    (b) his decisions
    (c) his little brother
    (d) Mr. Sawicki

48. Which of the following does NOT occur in the denouement?
    (a) King receives 25 years to life.
    (b) Cruz is sent to a reformatory after stealing a car.
    (c) Steve's father refuses to allow him to come home.
    (d) Steve begins to film himself, searching for his true identity.

C. Essay: Answer one of the following in a well-developed paragraph of at least five sentences. (10 pts.)

(a) Explain Steve Harmon's view of truth and innocence. Cite specific examples from the book.

(b) Explain whether you think Steve is innocent or guilty. Cite specific examples from the book.

(c) Explain whether or not you think *Monster* is an appropriate title for the book.

D. Creative Response: Choose one of the following. (6 pts.)

(a) Write a letter from Steve to Ms. O'Brien five years after the trial.

(b) Write a five-senses poem about FEAR.

Name ______________________________

A. Identification: Write the name of the person each phrase best identifies. (2 pts. each)

____________________ 1. Intense, probing; seeks retribution for crime victim

____________________ 2. White-haired; eloquent; defends against overpowering testimony

____________________ 3. Introspective, afraid; regrets unwise decisions; uncertain about future

____________________ 4. Trusting, positive; mentor

____________________ 5. Looks older than age; sloppy; the "Thug" of the story

____________________ 6. Young, well-built, articulate; first to find victim

____________________ 7. Petite; all business; probes into the defendant's background

____________________ 8. Big, mean, and ugly; the "Rat" of the story

____________________ 9. Juvenile gang member; the "Tough Guy Wannabe" of the story

____________________ 10. Retired school librarian; eyewitness at crime scene

B. Multiple Choice: Choose the BEST answer. (2 pts. each)

11. The movie script in *Monster* is designed to
    (a) portray life on the street
    (b) show the strong influence of family life
    (c) demonstrate how a few events can change a person's life forever
    (d) be used as a class project

12. O'Brien's task is to do all but which one of the following?
    (a) prove that King forced Steve to participate in the crime
    (b) make Steve a human being in the eyes of the jurors
    (c) make sure the law works for, not against, Steve
    (d) prove reasonable doubt that Steve was involved in the crime

13. The prosecution seeks to prove all but which one of the following?
    (a) Evans fired the gun that killed Nesbitt.
    (b) Osvaldo Cruz was to detain anyone who followed King and Evans.
    (c) Steve Harmon acted as the lookout.
    (d) Bobo Evans and James King perpetrated the crime.

14. Steve feels that Petrocelli is using Zinzi and Bolden's testimonies to
    (a) cast doubt on the validity of Cruz's testimony
    (b) remind the jury that Steve and King look just like Zinzi and Bolden
    (c) detract from the magnitude of the crime
    (d) implicate José Delgado in the crime
15. Steve's experiences in prison typify
    (a) the bravado with which a prisoner defends himself
    (b) the injustices of the penal system
    (c) that people take on the characteristics of those they are around
    (d) that juveniles should never be placed in prison with hardened criminals
16. O'Brien thinks that half the jury believed Steve was guilty as soon as they saw him for all but which of the following?
    (a) He is young.
    (b) He is on trial.
    (c) He is Black.
    (d) He has a Diablos tattoo.
17. Osvaldo Cruz is a paradox because of
    (a) his bravado and harshness on the street/his timidity and gentleness on the witness stand
    (b) his frightened demeanor/his membership in a gang
    (c) his age/his courage
    (d) his school record/his criminal record
18. Steve describes his presence in the drugstore by
    (a) reminding himself he was there to get medicine
    (b) convincing himself he was there to film activities for his school project
    (c) telling himself he was forced into the action by King
    (d) envisioning himself walking into the drugstore to look for mints, then walking out
19. Bobo Evans' testimony does all but which of the following?
    (a) identifies Steve Harmon as one of the participants in the crime
    (b) accuses King of firing the fatal shot
    (c) identifies Delgado as one of the participants in the crime
    (d) acknowledges he and King ate immediately after the murder
20. Briggs attacks Evans' credibility by stressing all but which one of the following?
    (a) He is a thief.
    (b) He is a gang leader.
    (c) He can see a man killed and immediately go eat.
    (d) He is a drug dealer.

Name ______________________________

21. O'Brien tells Steve he must
    (a) present himself as someone the jurors can believe in
    (b) deny he ever knew King or Evans
    (c) plead temporary insanity
    (d) plead guilty to a lesser charge
22. Which of the following is NOT true concerning Steve's testimony?
    (a) He denies any connection to the crime.
    (b) He admits he was at the drugstore that day but only to buy medicine.
    (c) He denies even being in the drugstore the day of the crime.
    (d) He acknowledges a casual acquaintance with King, Evans, and Cruz.
23. Mr. Sawicki's testimony in Steve's defense includes all but which one of the following?
    (a) He knows Steve was working on a film project the day of the crime.
    (b) He has known Steve for three years.
    (c) He thinks Steve is an outstanding young man.
    (d) Steve is very involved in depicting his neighborhood in a positive manner.
24. O'Brien's summation asserts that
    (a) King acted alone in committing the crime
    (b) it was impossible for her client to have been in the drugstore that day
    (c) the state has failed to prove her client even knew King
    (d) the state has failed to produce an eyewitness who can place Steve in the drugstore the day of the crime.
25. Steve does not want to think about
    (a) the fate of the inmates in prison
    (b) his own decisions
    (c) his film project
    (d) his future

C. Short Answer: Write brief answers for the following questions. (2 pts. each)

26. What mood does the initial scene of *Monster* establish?

27. What does the movie script in *Monster* reflect?

Name ______________________________

28. During the prosecutor's opening statements, what is Steve doing?

29. Why does Zinzi testify for the prosecution?

30. How does Detective Karyl portray Nesbitt?

31. What does O'Brien tell Steve they must show about Petrocelli?

32. What is the most critical point the defense reveals about Osvaldo Cruz?

33. What is the penalty Steve faces if he is convicted of the crime for which he is being tried?

34. How does Steve's father react when he visits Steve in prison?

35. How does Petrocelli attempt to impact the jury with the horror of the crime?

36. How did Mr. Nesbitt die?

37. Explain the irony of Jerry's visit to Steve.

38. Why does Bobo Evans agree to testify against King and Steve?

39. What would be Steve's advice to Jerry?

40. Explain what happens to the following in the denouement: Steve, King, Cruz.

D. Essay: Answer one of the following in a well-developed paragraph of at least seven sentences. (10 pts.)

(a) Support or refute the statement, "A person involved in any part of a murder is as guilty as the one who pulls the trigger."

(b) Sir Thomas Browne (1605-1682) stated, "Yet is every man his greatest enemy, and, as it were, his own executioner" (Browne. *Religio Medici*, Part II, Section 1. 1643). Correlate this statement with Steve Harmon's character in *Monster.*

E. Creative Response: Choose one of the following. (10 pts.)

(a) Write a diamente poem contrasting Guilt and Innocence.

(b) Rewrite the ending, beginning with the verdict.

Answer Key

Activities #1 & #2: Responses will vary.

Study Questions, Pages 1-19: *Responses to starred thought/opinion questions will vary.* 1. Steve Harmon; 16 years old; in jail; a few months; afraid and alone (pp. 1-5) 2. It is a survival technique; he is trying to make sense of what is happening to him; the movie will tell the story of his experience (pp. 4-5) 3. That is what the prosecutor calls him (p. 5). 4. Felony murder; O'Brien, his lawyer, tells Steve this is as serious as it gets and the prosecution is pushing for the death penalty; jury must realize Steve takes the trial as seriously as they do (pp. 12-13). 5. Activity **Pages 20-43:** 1. robbery of a drugstore; owner killed in struggle over gun; James King and Bobo Evans; lookout (pp. 21-24) 2. Five cartons of cigarettes were missing after the murder. A witness for the prosecution tells the court that while he was in jail, another inmate told him he had bought stolen cigarettes from a man involved in a drugstore robbery. The prosecutor ties these cigarettes to the crime (pp. 29-37). 3. Zinzi informs because he is afraid and wants to get out of prison. Both Briggs and O'Brien say he would do anything, including lie, to get out of prison (pp. 36-40). 4. Responses will vary, it may reveal how easily an innocent act can lead to trouble and show that Steve does not accept responsibility for his actions (p. 41). 5. Activity **Pages 45-58:** 1. hates jail; lives in fear (pp. 45-46) 2. witness for the prosecution who has been arrested for breaking and entering, possession of drugs with intent to sell, and assault; He exchanged the information he got from Bobo Evans for early release from jail (pp. 47-49, 52-55). 3. Steve has prior acquaintance with King; King had mentioned to Steve about robbing a drugstore; Steve comes from a strong family. 4. Responses will vary. **Pages 59-88:** 1. to let them look and sound terrible on the stand and then remind the jury that they don't look any different from Steve and King (p. 60) 2. Steve dreams he is in the courtroom trying to ask questions and, although he is shouting, no one can hear him and everyone goes about business as if Steve isn't there (p. 63). 3. Responses will vary. 4. Karyl describes the gruesome scene of the victim's death and tells about the missing cartons of cigarettes (pp. 67-69). 5. He received a tip from Zinzi about Bolden's purchase of stolen cigarettes; Bolden identified Evans and King, who implicated Steve (p. 70). 6. She says that nothing is happening that speaks to Steve's being innocent; she believes half of the jurors believed he was guilty from the first because he is young, Black, and on trial (p. 78). 7. member of Diablos gang; acts tough when on the street but subdued in the courtroom; identifies King and Steve in the courtroom and testifies that he agreed to join the others in the robbery because he is afraid of Bobo Evans, James King, and Steve Harmon (pp. 82-87). **Pages 89-113:** 1. Steve is discouraged because O'Brien feels the case is not going well; hearing prisoners discuss crimes and jail sentences causes him to think about his own possible jail term; guards torment him; death photos of Nesbitt torment him; fear overpowers everything else (pp. 89-98). 2. realizes the horror of Nesbitt's death; wants to see his reaction and try to find out who he really is (pp. 91-92) 3. Steve—lookout; Osvaldo—slow down anyone who pursued King and Evans when they left the store after the robbery (p. 100) 4. go to jail or put someone else in jail; Responses will vary (p. 104). 5. He lied about being a member of the Diablos; perhaps he will do anything, including lie, to better himself; willingly cut a stranger in the face as initiation into Diablos; got a girl other than his girlfriend pregnant; one juror shakes her head as if disgusted (pp. 105-109) 6. Responses will vary (pp. 110-113). 7. Activity **Pages 115-126:** 1. badly; she is afraid the jury won't see a difference between Steve and the other people who are taking the stand (p. 116). 2. He overhears a discussion about the crime between two women; he drops the basketball he is holding and runs (pp. 117-120). 3. Two armed and masked bandits rushed into Nesbitt's drugstore. When he was slow handing over the money, they killed him (p. 120). 4. Mother—disbelieving, alarmed, frightened; brother Jerry—reaches out toward Steve as detectives take him away; Father—anguished, crying with deep grief (pp. 124-125) 5. Activity **Pages 127-151:** 1. She makes sure the jury sees the crime scene photos of Nesbitt for the second time, just before the weekend recess (pp. 127-128).

2. He is one of five guys, all dressed exactly alike, all doing the same thing (pp. 128-129). 3. He wanted to be tough like the others (p. 130). 4. drowned in his own blood (p. 136) 5. He asks what she is going to do that weekend and, before responding, she gives him a funny look. To his question about how many times she has appeared in court, she replies "Too many times." Steve is convinced O'Brien thinks he is guilty. To his avowed, "I'm not guilty," she replies, "You should have said, 'I didn't do it.'" (pp. 137-138). 6. Steve thinks he isn't guilty because he just walked in the drugstore to look for some mints, then walked back out. He didn't kill Mr. Nesbitt (p. 140). 7. Her tears make Steve realize the terrible effect his being in jail has on her. They visit about everyday things, she questions her choice of a lawyer, tells him she will bring Jerry the next day, and brings him a Bible. She vows her belief in his innocence and her love for him. He feels her pain intensely and can hardly make it back to his cell. He wonders if he is fooling himself about his innocence (pp. 144-148). 8. Activity **Pages 153-171:** 1. All the inmates have going for them in jail is surface stuff such as how people look at them and what they say, so they have to protect those rights (pp. 154-155). 2. Jerry isn't allowed in the visiting area of the jail because he is too young. Steve would also be too young to come into the visiting room if he were not locked up (p. 156). 3. She was in the drugstore the day of the crime and identifies James King as one of two men she heard arguing with Mr. Nesbitt about the money just before he was killed (pp. 161-171). 4. He brings out the point that she didn't recognize King at first from the photographs and implies that the police manipulated her into identifying King, both in the pictures and in the lineup (pp. 166-170). 5. She says she has trouble testifying against a Black man (p. 169). 6. Activity **Pages 172-200:** 1. because he is in prison uniform; doesn't think it will make a difference and rules against the objection (pp. 172-173) 2. Greenhaven; 7 1/2 to 10 years; selling drugs; breaking and entering, grand theft auto, stealing a car radio, manslaughter (pp. 175-176) 3. He and King planned the robbery and Steve acted as lookout. He and King got into an argument with Nesbitt, who pulled a gun on them and started shooting. They struggled and King accidentally killed Nesbitt. He implies the shooting was accidental. They took some cigarettes and money, left, bought food, and split the rest of the money. 4. as a manipulative, self-interested dope dealer and a thief who is trying to "cop a plea" in the robbery/murder charge; as a cold-hearted criminal who can see a man killed and then have a good meal from a fast-food place 5. Activity **Pages 201-214:** 1. O'Brien: separate Steve from James King; Briggs: make sure jury connects King and Steve because Steve looks like a decent guy (p. 201) 2. scared, disheartened, anxious, overwhelmed, crushed; believes O'Brien thinks they've lost the case; his heart beating like crazy, he has trouble breathing (pp. 201-203) 3. Dorothy Moore; King brought her a lamp and was with her the afternoon of the crime (pp. 206-209) 4. to show that King is left-handed; implication is that since Nesbitt's wound was on the left side of body, he was probably shot by a right-handed person (pp. 211-214) 5. Activity **Pages 215-237:** 1. to take the stand in his own defense, trying to break the link between himself and King and present himself as someone in whom the jurors can believe (p. 215-216) 2. denies being in the drugstore the day of the crime or being involved in the robbery in any way; acknowledges visiting casually with King and Cruz and possibly speaking with Evans (pp. 223-230) 3. The prosecution can prove King lied when he said he didn't know Bobo Evans (p. 216). 4. only on television (p. 217) 5. Steve: what you know to be right; Inmates: one doesn't know what truth is and thinks it is the prosecutor's way of looking for a way to stick you under the jail; other, something you gave up on the street (pp. 221-222) 6. Bobo's testimony that Steve came out of the drugstore just before the robbery and Cruz's testimony that he was told Steve was supposed to be the lookout (pp. 228-231) 7. says he was going around different places the day of the crime, making mental notes for a school film project (pp. 231-232) **Pages 238-253:** 1. Briggs presents Bobo Evans as an undesirable character who is capable of anything and who implicates King because the police have offered him a deal (pp. 238-239). 2. (1) questions Bobo's motives for testifying (2) alludes to Bobo's undesirable character (3) questions Lorelle Henry's concentration on the day of the crime and the method by which she picked

King's pictures (4) restates King's alibi (5) questions "parade" of admitted criminals as prosecution's witnesses (6) questions Cruz's reason for testifying (pp. 238-243) 3. (1) acknowledges medical examiner's testimony that a murder has been committed but stresses he does not indicate who is responsible (2) states that Steve was not in the store, it was not his gun, and he did not converse with King about the crime (3) states that Henry was in the store but was not reported by a lookout (4) says Bobo testified there was no signal (5) says only Bobo and King ate and split the money after the crime (6) questions reliability of testimony of Cruz and King (7) stresses Steve's good character (8) alludes to reasonable doubt (pp. 244-253) 4. Activity **Pages 254-281:** 1. (1) refocuses away from character of witnesses (2) reexamines witnesses' testimony (3) states that three witnesses placed King in the store the day of the crime (4) refers to sale of cigarettes (5) gives state's theory of what happened (6) attacks Steve's character because of his association with King (pp. 254-262) 2. Opinion—Responses will vary but may refer to Washington's reputation for truthfulness, the importance of justice under state and national jurisdiction (pp. 263-264) 3. Steve Harmon: found not guilty, released; James King: found guilty and sentenced to 25 years to life; Bobo Evans: still in jail; Cruz: arrested for stealing a car and sent to a reformatory (pp. 279-280) 4. makes movies of himself talking to the camera, and says he is searching for his true identity (pp. 280-281) 5. Responses will vary.

Activity #3: 1.d 2. m 3. h 4. g 5. k 6. j 7. b 8. l 9. t 10. c 11. q 12. n 13. r 14. a 15. o 16. i 17. s 18. e 19. f 20. p **Activity #4:** Charts will vary. Definitions: 1. affidavit: written statement or oath 2. pans: to move a motion picture or television camera either vertically or horizontally, so as to take in a larger scene or to follow a moving object 3. grotesque: distorted, absurd 4. pessimist: one who has the tendency to see the worst side of things 5. lethal: deadly, fatal 6. grimaces: to make distorted, wry faces 7. perpetrator: one who commits something bad 8. proposition: statement or assertion; suggestion of terms 9. juvenile: young person, child 10. civil: polite, courteous 11. judicial: of judges; having to do with a law court or the administration of justice 12. apprehended: taking hold of; seized by authority 13. ruffled: annoyed, put out 14. hexagon: figure with six sides 15. cope: contend, deal with 16. cacophony: disagreeable sound; discord of sounds 17. ghetto: part of a city where members of a particular minority group predominate or are restricted 18. dismay: consternation, horrified amazement 19. glowers: scowls; stares angrily or fiercely 20. precinct: division of a city as relates to policing and voting **Activity #5:** Sentences will vary; guide offers suggestions. 1. No—The arcs of light traveled in curves. 2. Yes 3. Yes 4. No—The perimeter outlines the outer boundary of the figure. 5. Yes 6. No—The trapezius is in the upper area of the body. 7. No—The policeman forcibly wrenched the gun from the suspect. 8. Yes 9. No—Playing whist requires cards. 10. No—Diminutive basketball players would usually be too small to play in a professional league. 11. Yes 12. No—A prejudicial witness is considered hostile and is usually detrimental to the case. 13. No—Manslaughter is the murder of someone without deliberate intent on the part of the perpetrator. 14. Yes 15. Yes 16. No - You would not expect hurdy-gurdy music in a church. **Activity #6:** 1. d 2. h 3. k 4. a 5. c 6. g 7. j 8. b 9. f 10. l 11. i 12. e **Activity #7:** 1. Contention 2. taint 3. implicates 4. moral 5. reformatory 6. causative 7. gullible 8. botched 9. potential 10. acquit 11. elicit 12. Consigning 13. pensive 14. indulgence 15. Dialog 16. constitute 17. bravado 18. alleged **Activities #8-#15:** *Responses will vary. This key gives suggested responses.* **Activity #8:** Center circle: Steve Harmon; smaller circles and lines: needs—peace of mind, freedom from fear, an acquittal; regrets—listening to King, being involved in robbery, wanting to be like King and Evans; loves—his parents, Jerry; excels—in film-making class; fears—jail, other inmates, his own thoughts; seeks—understanding of himself, O'Brien's approval. **Activity #9:** Central Oval: The Trial; Characters and their reactions: Steve—fear, anxiety, apprehension; O'Brien—concern, apprehension; Petrocelli—confidence, animosity; King—anger, uncertainty, insolence; Evans—anger, belligerence; Cruz—disdain, subservience, hostility. **Activity #10:** Steve Harmon: 16 years old, good student, strong family life, easily led, desires to be

"tough," regrets wrong decisions, afraid of jail. King: criminal, cruel, manipulative, self-serving. Evans: criminal, heartless, belligerent, concerned only about himself, plea-bargains to get lesser charge. Cruz: tough when around peers, weak when confronted with charges, vicious, member of Diablos gang, self-serving. Kathy O'Brien: Steve's attorney, decisive, thorough, uncertain about outcome of trial, probingly looks at Steve. Sandra Petrocelli: prosecutor, confident, probing, astute, determined to get conviction for Steve and King. Steve's parents: good parents, filled with sorrow and apprehension, can't understand how Steve got mixed up with King and Evans. Mr. Sawicki: Steve's mentor in film club, strong role model, views Steve as honest, hardworking student, willing to testify in his defense. **Activity #11:** (1) Steve Harmon allegedly becomes involved with two criminals, King and Evans, and is their lookout for a drugstore robbery. (2) During the robbery, Mr. Nesbitt, the owner of the drugstore, is killed. (3) Steve is arrested, placed in jail, and charged with felony murder. (4) Steve and James King are tried for the crime at the same time. The prosecutor attempts to prove they are both guilty although King fired the fatal shot. (5) The jury convicts King but acquits Steve. **Activity #12:** Book: *Monster*. Main Characters: Steve Harmon, James King, Bobo Evans, Osvaldo Cruz, Kathy O'Brien, Asa Briggs, Sandra Petrocelli. Minor Characters: The Judge, Lorelle Henry, Bolden, Zinzi, José Delgado, Mr. Sawicki, Dorothy Moore, Mr. and Mrs. Harmon. Themes: fear, self-perception, guilt/innocence. Setting: Manhattan Detention Center, New York City courtroom, Harlem. Point of View: first-person narration. Genre: fiction. Conflict: Steve Harmon vs. James King, Bobo Evans, and Osvaldo Cruz, Steve vs. himself, Steve vs. the judicial system. Author's style and tone: sincere, original narrative that interweaves journal entries and courtroom proceedings in screenplay format; informal, somber tone. **Activity #13:** Effect: Self-perception. Causes: (1) Steve Harmon attempts to be as tough as King and Evans. (2) The prosecutor refers to him as "monster." (3) While in jail on charges of felony murder, he experiences overwhelming fear of the other inmates and for his own future. (4) He searches for the truth within himself: his guilt or innocence. (5) He reflects on his promising future as a filmmaker and the respect of his mentor. (6) He searches for what O'Brien sees in him that causes her to turn away from him. **Activity #14:** Problem: Steve Harmon must decide whether or not to join King, Evans, and Cruz in the robbery. Choices: (1) Join them. (2) Ignore them. (3) Tell his parents. (4) Report them to the police. (5) Agree to participate but just not show up. (6) Try to talk them out of the robbery. Criteria: (1) Will he wind up in trouble? (2) Will the boys leave him alone? (3) Will the police think he is part of the group? (4) Can this possibly stop the crime? (5) Will anyone believe him? **Activity #15:** Dialogue on pp. 110-113. Steve and his dad are speaking. Plot advanced by showing uncertainty of the outcome of the trial and impact of Steve's imprisonment on his family. Special because it expresses Mr. Harmon's hopes for his son's future, his uncertainty about Steve's involvement in the crime, and his struggle to believe everything will be all right. The dialogue reveals the deep reciprocal love between Mr. Harmon and Steve. Mr. Harmon loves his son unconditionally, and Steve feels deep remorse for the pain he is causing his family. **Activity #16, Quiz 1:** 1. d 2. e 3. a 4. c 5. b 6. T (pp. 1-4) 7. F (p. 4) 8. T (pp. 10, 22) 9. T (pp. 48-49) 10. F (pp. 22-23) **Activity #17, Quiz 2:** 1. monster (p. 61) 2. human (pp. 62-63) 3. James King (p. 71) 4. nothing is happening that speaks of Steve's innocence, jury may not see a difference between Steve and all the bad guys taking the stand 5. young, Black, on trial (p. 79) 6. Diablos (pp. 81, 106) 7. he was afraid of Bobo Evans, James King, and Steve Harmon (p. 87) 8. 25 years to life (p. 90) 9. lookout (p. 100) 10. accusing him of lying to stay out of jail; pointing out his willingness to fight and hurt others to get into the Diablos; beating his girlfriend (pp. 104-109) 11. in his home (pp. 124-125) **Activity #18, Quiz 3:** 1. T (p. 127) 2. F (p. 131) 3. F (pp. 135-136) 4. F (pp. 156-157) 5. T (p. 187) 6. wonders what is wrong with walking in the drugstore, then walking out; knows that he didn't kill Mr. Nesbitt (p. 140) 7. No matter what anyone says, she knows he's innocent and she loves him very much (pp. 147-148).
8. She was in the drugstore just prior to the crime and identifies King as being present (pp. 161-164).
9. says he and King planned and enacted the robbery; murder was not intentional; identifies King and

Steve (pp. 177-179) 10. He was afraid of Bobo Evans (p. 192). **Activity #19, Quiz 4:** 1. Mr. Sawicki's (p. 204) 2. she is his cousin (pp. 206-209, 217) 3. separate himself from King; present himself as someone the jurors can believe in (p. 216) 4. drilling him in a game with a cup: up for good answers, down for bad (p. 218) 5. "No, I was not" (p. 224) 6. F (p. 215) 7. T (p. 217) 8. F (pp. 225-228) 9. F (p. 231) 10. T (p. 235)

Activity #20, Quiz 5: 1. B (p. 252) 2. C (p. 262) 3. E (p. 270) 4. C (p. 257) 5. A (p. 242) 6. E (pp. 279-281) 7. D (p. 276) 8. A (p. 240) 9. B (pp. 276, 281) 10. E (p. 276)

Final Test, Level One

A. 1. e 2. c 3. g 4. i 5. l 6. a 7. h 8. j 9. b 10. k 11. f 12. d

B. 13. c (pp. 1-5) 14. a (throughout book) 15. d (p. 12) 16. b (p. 20) 17. c (p. 22) 18. b (p. 24) 19. d (pp. 29-31) 20. a (p. 40) 21. d (pp. 48-53) 22. c (p. 58) 23. a (p. 60) 24. b (p. 62) 25. d (p. 72) 26. c (p. 79) 27. a (p. 106) 28. b (p. 87) 29. a (p. 90) 30. c (pp. 96, 130) 31. d (p. 100) 32. b (p. 101) 33. a (pp. 111-113) 34. d (p. 127) 35. c (p. 136) 36. b (p. 140) 37. b (p. 146) 38. d (p. 164) 39. a (p. 167) 40. c (pp. 178-179) 41. d (pp. 185-187) 42. b (p. 187) 43. c (p. 201) 44. d (p. 205) 45. a (p. 234) 46. d (pp. 245-248) 47. b (p. 260) 48. c (pp. 279-281)

C & D: Responses will vary.

Final Test, Level Two

A. 1. Sandra Petrocelli 2. Asa Briggs 3. Steve Harmon 4. Mr. Sawicki 5. James King 6. José Delgado 7. Kathy O'Brien 8. Bobo Evans 9. Osvaldo Cruz 10. Lorelle Henry

B. 11. c (p. 9) 12. a (pp. 16, 20, 26) 13. a (p. 22) 14. b (p. 60) 15. c (p. 62) 16. d (p. 79) 17. a (pp. 80-82) 18. d (p. 140) 19. c (p. 40) 20. b (p. 187) 21. a (p. 216) 22. b (pp. 223-231) 23. a (p. 234) 24. d (pp. 245-248) 25. b (p. 270)

C. 26. fear (pp. 1-5) 27. Steve Harmon's search for his true self 28. writing the word "monster" over and over (p. 24) 29. in order to get out of jail early (p. 40) 30. hard-working, well-respected Black man (p. 72) 31. She simply made a mistake (p. 79). 32. He lied about being a member of the Diablos gang (p. 106). 33. 25 years to life (p. 90) 34. cries with anguish and sorrow (pp. 111-113) 35. She shows them graphic pictures of the victim just before the weekend (p. 127). 36. drowned in his own blood (p. 136) 37. Jerry can't visit Steve inside the jail because he is too young. If Steve were not an inmate in the jail, he would also be too young to visit (p. 156). 38. as a plea bargain for a lesser charge with shorter sentence (pp. 185-187) 39. think about all the tomorrows of his life (p. 205) 40. Steve: found innocent; King: found guilty, sentenced to 25 years to life; Cruz: sent to reformatory for stealing a car (pp. 279-281)

D & E: Responses will vary.

Notes